100 WAYS
TO IMPROVE TEACHING
USING YOUR
VOICE & MUSIC

---

*Pathways to
Accelerate Learning*

---

by Don G. Campbell

D1473479

Zephyr
Press

Tucson, Arizona

Other books and tapes by Don G. Campbell

Books:
The Roar of Silence. Quest Books, 1989.
Master Teacher, Nadia Boulanger. Pastoral Press, 1984.
Introduction to the Musical Brain. Magna Music, 1983.
Music: Physician for Times to Come. Quest Books, 1991.
Rhythms of Learning: Creative Tools for Developing Lifelong Skills
(with Chris Brewer). Zephyr Press, 1991.
Music and Miracles. Quest Books, 1992.

Sound Cassettes:
Healing Yourself with Your Own Voice. Sounds True, 1990.
Cosmic Classics. Spirit Music, Inc., 1988.
Crystal Rainbows. Spirit Music, Inc., 1985.
Angels. Greater Spiral, 1985.
Lightning on the Moon. Greater Spiral, 1985.
Crystal Meditations. Spirit Music, Inc., 1984.
Sound Pathways: Using Your Voice and Music to Accelerate Learning.
Zephyr Press, 1992.

100 WAYS TO IMPROVE TEACHING
USING YOUR VOICE AND MUSIC
Pathways to Accelerate Learning

Grades K–Adult

© 1992 Zephyr Press

ISBN: 0-913705-74-8

Editor: Stacey Lynn
Cover Design: Michelle Gallardo
Book Design and Production: Nancy Taylor

Zephyr Press
P.O. Box 66006
Tucson, AZ 85728-6006

Dedicated to Michael Alexander and the faculty of the Simon Guggenheim School in the inner city of Chicago.

CONTENTS

This book is like a wonderful waterfall of ideas.

It flows and rushes with creative ways to use your own voice to improve your unique style of communication.

This is a SOUND handbook with a hundred pathways for developing a better ear, a versatile voice, and stronger intuition for teaching and training.

You need not be a musician to use the benefits of music.

Allow a natural tolerance for joy and beauty to develop.

Continuity and contrast, connectedness and variety make learning and teaching successful. Sound is a magic bridge.

Start anywhere, blend techniques with your personality, and listen, listen, **listen**, listen as you speak! You'll see and hear results!

PREFACE

More than five years ago, I received a call from a principal of an inner-city school in Chicago who said, "I've seen you teach! Can you come here and show the teachers in my school how to do what you do?"

Michael Alexander knew about accelerated learning; he allowed creativity, enthusiasm, and heart to live in children, teachers, and methods. I knew after my first visit to the school that multisensory integrated methods in accelerated learning would work at the Guggenheim. Through these techniques and the wisdom of the teachers, administration, students, and parents, Guggenheim is a miracle story. Peter Clines, Lyle Palmer, Nancy Ellis, Lybian Cassonne, Dee Dickinson, and many other trainers have helped Michael Alexander bring a vision into reality.

A group of inner-city teachers became my teachers. All the years of learning brain theory, creative development, and music were put to the test, and their enthusiasm and honesty strengthened and raised my own emotional and social IQ.

What follows are the creative and cream-of-the-crop exercises that came from the Guggenheim School, the "Sound Business" projects that use voice and music in corporate training, and the brainstorms with hundreds of teachers who have shared intuitive methods with me.

The importance of left-brain theory is essential but put aside in this book. Whether you have a great deal of creative, multisensorial, and integrated brain methods or if you are just beginning with a few simple exercises to test the water you can use *100 Ways!*

My recent book, created with Chris Brewer, *Rhythms of Learning* (Zephyr Press, 1991), provides an important foundation in educational theories and practices. It provides a context in which this book can be seen as logical and consistent with brain development and memory. *Rhythms* provides the basic introduction to the important research and work of Dr. A. A. Tomatis in France and Dr. Georgi Lozanov in Bulgaria.

An earlier book, *Introduction to the Musical Brain* (MagnaMusic, 1983), provides the creative, right brain approach to childhood education. For teachers who use music, it is a brainstorm of practical activities and associative exercises and activities.

Lifelong learning is not a dreamy idea. Our general health, sense of well-being, and self-esteem are dependent on the way we learn to integrate the inner and outer worlds. Start on any page, mix and match, then create your own unique style for improving communication, listening, and learning through your voice and music.

A hundred thanks to the hundred people who helped me experiment with new ways to make the voice, ear, and brain dance! Among them: Jean Houston, Chris Brewer, Larry Dossey, Bob Samples, Joseph Chilton Pierce, Elaine de Beauport, Barbara Clark, Barbara Given, Libyan Cassonne, Alfred Tomatis, Lena Tomatis, Billie Thompson, Judith Belk, Dee Coulter, Paul Maduale, Barbara Crowe, Diane Davalos, Diana Butler, Lynn Larson, John Cardwell, Jonathan Goldman, and Kitaro.

1 The Pour-On Technique

My father was from Arkansas. He had remarkably simple and funny ways of being wise. One of the things he said to me as a child, then as a young man, and later as an adult was: "Don, if you can't **pour** it **on** 'em, then pour it where it will run on 'em."

Years later, I realized Dad's "pour-on" wisdom was the basis of multisensory, intuitive education. To realize that we can use many different modalities to present information is a key for being understood. Every student and teacher has a different way of integrating sensory experience. The more opportunities our "output" creates for better listening, seeing, sensing, and feeling, the better and more interesting it is for the learner.

Speak aloud something you do well in a teaching situation and invent three variations on it. Use your voice to make the variations and test them. You may discover even better styles. The rest of the book is filled with "pour-on" tests!

2 Triple-Coding

Whatever you are teaching, think of three different sensory modes that will present the materials. These questions are helpful in learning how to **triple-code** a concept:

- Did the learner hear me?

- Did the learner see what I meant?

- Could the learner repeat what I said in his/her imagination? Could he/she write it down?

- Did I present the material with visual clarity?

- Did I speak clearly the information I was teaching?

- Did I review the information while the learner was relaxed?

- Did I review the information in an alert, active style?

When techniques, methods, and information are "triple-coded," high-yield memory is far more available than with single mode memory association.

Optimize the opportunity for remembering a variety of auditory, visual, imaginary, relaxed, and active styles when presenting information. Don't forget texture, touch, and fragrance when you need variety in triple-coding.

3 *Speak Easy*

Speaking is music. It has a rhythm, a pace. It is carried by tonal sounds and holds information and emotions. Even when there is silence between words or between sentences, the beat goes on.

Somewhere you've got some cassette tapes with speeches, lectures, or sermons. Listen to three or four minutes of a speaker that you enjoy. The pace may get slightly faster or slower, but generally professional speakers intuitively keep a pace.

Begin to notice the rhythmic patterns in voices. Try to tap a constant rhythm underneath their speech. Listen for regularity in the pace. Notice if the voice pattern changes during a very interesting part of a presentation.

4 *Listen, Listen, Listen*

Ready, set, let's just jump into the middle of the Real Stuff!

Tape one of your classes or presentations. Listen to the tape and answer the following questions:

- Did I sense enthusiasm in my voice?

- When was it greatest?

- Did I speak at the same pace throughout the class?

- Did my voice change throughout the class?

To see and to hear may be a little too much at once, but give this exercise a try. It may feel awkward if you are shy, a perfectionist, or terribly critical. Nevertheless, this suggestion is a biggie! Let's do it soon and then everything else gets easy and much more fun.

After you listen to the tape, note one suggestion you have for adding some variety to your voice when there is a lack of enthusiasm. In the following dozen exercises you'll discover some specific techniques for improving enthusiasm and variation in the voice.

5 *Variety Is the Spice of Life*

Variety in speech patterns allows listeners to be more engaged and retain more information from a speaker. A voice that has no variation in pace, pattern, or inflection becomes boring very quickly. (Remember that college teacher who could put you to sleep in two minutes ?)

Too much emotional variation in a voice can make it difficult to receive the factual information that is being presented. Vocal variation is like seasoning in the kitchen. Bland is boring, and too much spice can make the result indigestible.

Go back to the tape of yourself. Give yourself a report on the spices you hear in your voice. Too much emotion? Too little enthusiasm? Just right on the accents? Make a list of three things you can do to spice up or spice down your teaching and presentations. (Remember to triple-code!)

6 *Loudmouth Listening*

Have you ever noticed a person in your class who speaks louder than everyone else? Have you ever been caught off guard in a restaurant when suddenly you're speaking so loudly that everyone in the restaurant turns to look at you?

Often a loud voice is produced by a hearing deficiency. We literally and physically need to hear ourselves think. Speaking actually charges our brain and gives us a positive physical sensation. (Remember Aunt Bertha, who just talked and talked and talked? She didn't listen—she just babbled! That was an important release of tension for her.)

Next time you are in conversation with a person whose voice is loud, slow down your pace a little, and quiet your voice just a little. If the other person talks louder, it could mean there is a slight hearing impairment. If he or she slows down a little and becomes a little quieter, you know they are listening and able to change their listening and speaking patterns.

What Did You Say?

Public speaking is one of the great fear producers in our culture. Many of us are simply shy when it comes to speaking our mind and our feelings.

Often voices are so light and so shy that we cannot hear what is being said. It is possible that people with shy voices actually have very sensitive hearing and sound has an invading quality for them.

Find a safe time before or after a class to speak with the shy voice. Without changing your natural voice, just speak with a little quieter voice and ask if your voice range is comfortable for the class. "Am I speaking too loudly or too softly for you?" Notice if your listeners' voices change as they respond.

8 *Just Charge It!*

Dr. Alfred Tomatis, a remarkable French physician and researcher, has discovered that some voices make "charged" sounds. They invigorate and bring attention to both the speaker and the listener. Charged sounds do not have to be loud or emotional, but they are radiant and full.

"Uncharged" sounds drain the body of life, make information boring, and disengage mind from body. No matter what the information is, it does not feel real to the mind or the body.

Imagine that your whole body is a sounding board and that it is fully participating in your speech. Allow yourself to feel relaxation in your jaw. Then stretch with a couple of yawns and a minute of resonant humming—yes, just hum with a full sound. This exercise is invaluable. It easily unlocks the power of the voice.

9 *Out of Phase*

Sometimes we are just "out of phase" or "offbeat" with a student or colleague. Our words and intentions just are not communicating and we feel helpless.

It could actually be that our human instruments are built very differently in terms of rhythm and breath. By making an effort to enter into the other person's pace, rhythm, and sound, we may be able to communicate more easily.

Before you speak, take five to ten seconds to notice if the listener's breath is shallow or deep. Let your breath match his or her breath. In other words, deepen your breath or "shallow" your breath and keep the same pace. This need be neither outwardly obvious nor precise. Gently "phase in" with them. Now you are a step closer in matching brain waves and the real physical "vibrations."

10 *Get It Right*

Nearly half the people in the world change their voice response depending on which of their ears receives the information. Research on over a million ears (that's 500,000 people) suggests that the best ear to use when you want to retain logical information is the right ear. (It's got the quickest grabs on the left brain.)

Position yourself on the left side of the room, so that your voice reaches the right ears of the listeners. You'll soon realize who the "lefties" and "righties" are. Watch out—being left-handed doesn't mean that there is always "left ear-ness" or that the heart has migrated to the right side of the body.

Here are some easy ways to keep your right ear stimulated:

- Use your right hand to hold the telephone to your right ear.

- In a classroom or office, have students or clients sit on your right side. That provides both of you with the right side advantage.

- Listen to classical or baroque music on a good stereo system or through a head set with the right side louder than the left.

11 Smooth, Rich, but Not Thick

In your private, sacred inner sanctum where no one in the universe will hear you, begin to experiment with your voice. See and hear what it can do.

You might be haunted by the great, awful plague of "feeling silly." This could be caused by someone saying to you in your early years, "Sit down, be quiet, and learn." Or even, "Keep a stiff upper lip." Try that one if you really want to feel silly!

Make up a phrase and then say it in ten different styles. Here's a great statement to try when you are driving. "Rush hour gives me a chance to slow down and relax after a day's work. I enjoy breathing deeply and listening to music."

- Say it as if you were a general giving orders.

- Say it as if you were yawning.

- Say it as if you were an evangelical preacher wanting the world to know about it!

- Say it with a drawl, like a slow, deep-voiced Texas oil man.

- Say it in the style of someone in a New York kosher deli.

- Say it with anger.

- Say it quietly, using the upper part of your voice, as if you're speaking to a baby.

- Create your own styles.

12 *In Harmony*

Neurolinguistic programming speaks of "rapport" as being essential in communication. Rapport makes us feel safe, heard, and part of a learning experience.

In music therapy, the same activity is called "entrainment." To be able to be a prime listener—without an "agenda" except patience, receptivity, and the ability to walk in the place of the other person—is healing. It brings trust and a sense of well-being.

We can learn to sense (really listen to) our students and associates. We can pace our energy, our voice, and our goals for communication based on "where they are." Then we can move on to a more relaxed or a more invigorated state.

Pay attention to the general rhythm and energy of your listeners. After lunch they will be slower, need a little more space, be inclined to daydream or go to sleep. A two- or three-minute period of listening to very slow classical music can give permission for the body and mind to just rest—before a lecture, for example. (There are many exercises coming up that will help you select music.) It's a great investment and it's refreshing—far better than fighting to stay awake.

13 *You Are Already a Musician*

It doesn't matter if you know about Mozart or how to play a guitar or if you like to sing, you are still very much a musician. Your heart beats all the time. It may speed up or slow down, but it has a continuous beat. Also, you breathe regularly. Your breath is consistent and has a rhythm.

You have dozens of other rhythms in your body: brain waves, stomach pulses, spinal fluid tides, eyes blinking—just to name a few. Every movement in the body's blood, muscle, and thought has rhythm.

Percussion students sometimes spend a whole lifetime trying to reproduce the natural and very complex rhythms that are in the body.

Listening to three minutes of rhythmic music at the beginning of class allows everyone's breathing and heartbeat to synchronize. To begin a class on the same wave length is optimal. Closing the eyes and listening to a Sousa march, the theme from *Flashdance*, or Scott Joplin's "The Entertainer" will allow the inner musician to jog, breathe, or dance with freedom in rhythm with others in the room.

14 Table Turning— with a Round Table

Being able to hear our own voice in many styles and ranges is very important. It is awkward to put on unfamiliar clothes, eat strange food, or go to concerts of music that we don't like. Making new sounds and exploring the voice are easy and fun with children. The older we become, the stranger it seems to experiment with accents and the voice.

Most of the exercises in this book are for you, but this is a table turner. It will give you courage for your own experimentation.

Give an assignment to your class to find two lines of a song or a poem to memorize. Then have them prepare three very different and interesting ways to say the same text. Here are some suggestions:

- Say it in rhythm or "rap" it.
- Say it like a giant would.
- Say it as if you were a little hummingbird.
- Make a melody with the words and sing it.
- Make it sound "stupid."
- Make it sound like a very wise old man or old woman.

15 *Table Turning— the Bored Room*

A friend of mine got a memo from her supervisor that said, "10:30 A.M. Bored Meeting in the Bored Room."

That was the first interesting meeting she had been to in a long time. Just the ability to express new ideas with vibrant enthusiasm can greatly change a meeting.

Next time you are in a meeting and wish to comment, imagine yourself doing one of the following:

- Clearly, simply, and happily finding the last piece in a grand jigzaw puzzle before you speak.

- Playing an instrument in a large symphony orchestra; you've just finished playing an inspiring melody.

- Whistling a happy tune on the inside as you speak.

Be gentle on yourself. This exercise might have originated with some of the most successful corporate managers in the world.

16 *Go with the Flow*

Patterns build, create, and inspire. Mental, physical and emotional patterns make us strong, clear, and focused. Creativity is the introduction of new patterns into our way of thinking and doing. Creativity is always risky!

Handel (baroque) and Haydn (classical) were very patterned musicians. They were not the experimenters of their musical periods. They polished styles but didn't do anything radical to the ears of their performers or audiences.

They were creative. They added ornaments to their melodies. Handel used trills, mordents, and interesting accents to decorate his melodies. He went with the flow but elegantly decorated the music that delights listeners.

Listen to Handel's *Water Music* or *Fireworks Music.* Notice how beautifully the music is organized. Listen for variations in the music-melodies played on various instruments, melodies played higher to lower, melodies and instruments that talk back and forth to each other.

Picture yourself teaching, and as you listen to the music, observe what easy and natural ornaments you can add to your presentation.

17 I . . . So . . . Principle

This title comes from the word *isoprinciple*, which is used often by music therapists.

Don't be concerned if you're not familiar with music therapy. It is an important emerging field in creative health studies. There are nearly five thousand therapists around the country using music to assist in nonmusical areas of growth, development, and health.

Isoprinciples are concerned with pacing, patterning, and the tempo (speed) of sound. They involve gradual changes in the speed of voice, music, or information presentation.

Tell a story and concentrate on beginning your speech in a slow, clear manner. Then gradually speak faster and faster. Reverse the process—start by speaking very quickly and then slow down gradually. The slow change of pace can dramatically affect the listener's attention.

18 Happy Birthday to YOU

The most popular song in the Western world really slows us down and ages us instantly. It is rarely sung at a constant tempo. Watch the words and inwardly sing the tune:

Hap py birth – day to you

Hap py birth – day to you

Hap py b i r t h d a y

D e a r t e a c h e r,

H a p p y b i r t h d a y

T o y o u !

When you want a class to slow down its pace, breath together and just lighten a frantic pace, find a birthday and sing the birthday song!

(P.S. This uses the isoprinciple technique!)

19 Bolero *with* NO BULL

Maurice Ravel was an inspired impressionist composer. He wrote some of the most beautiful and descriptive of all music. His most popular piece was written to describe the building of intensity in the bullfight. A bolero is a Spanish dance form that has this underlying rhythm:

After you've heard the melody a couple of times, you'll notice how lightly and slowly it begins, then gradually builds into a fiery, vibrant celebration.

When you want to charge yourself—to get out of bed in the morning or empower that sleepy afternoon time—take a twelve minute dose of "accelerated isoprinciple" with Ravel's *Bolero*. It works every time, no bull!

20 SSSSSSSSSSSS

For a hundred years teachers and parents have been making the "SSSSSShhhhhhhhh . . ." sound to invite silence or to stimulate attention. We know it's not always the most polite way to calm a class. But it is such a natural sound and it actually does work pretty well. Why? Because you are producing "white noise." The "ssshhhh . . ." has the highest frequencies that we can easily create with our voice and the sound can be heard over most speaking voices. Even nicer words like "hu<u>sh</u>" and "<u>si</u>lence" have the same high sounds that work.

Create some new words with the "ssssss" sound. Take words or phrases and prolong the "sssss" sound. For example, "Lissssssssssten"; "SSSSSSSound up !"

21 *Sibilant Rivalry*

Language specialists have long realized that the consonants hold the clarity and preciseness in most words. The sibilants, the high "sss" sound, and many of the consonants can be accentuated to improve diction.

Dr. Tomatis is aware that the sibilants and the highest sounds in our words are the most charged sounds, even to the unborn child. In rooms with carpet and air conditioners, and even with outside sounds, your communication will be improved if you polish your consonants.

Read a few selected paragraphs and leave out all the vowel sounds. Accentuate the tongue, lips, and face to see if you can still be understood. A great game for little folks is to speak a nursery rhyme without any vowel tones. This exercise helps enunciation!

22 *Vowel Movements*

The tone and sounds of vowels give expression to our voices. The emotional content of language can be sensed by the accents, rise, and fall of the vowel sounds that carry words into the world. Every language and every dialect has its own tonality, length, and color of vowels.

Read aloud and leave out all the consonants. (Yes, I know these exercises seem a bit silly around the edges, but they are tested through and through. They will develop more variety in your speaking voice.) The omissions automatically create a more emotive sound. The tonal (vowel) richness in the voice increases vocal power.

23 *A Free Tune-Up*

Some ears can match pitch easier than others. Off-pitch singers have been called monotones. Unfortunately, some of us go through life thinking that we cannot sing in tune.

Good news for every teacher, student, and sing-alonger is at hand. Depending on which ear hears the sound, the voice responds differently. The position of the eyes and how strongly the sound vibrates the bones in the skull also determine pitch.

Here are some "ears-on" techniques that can help you tune up a student's voice.

- Sing a long "oouuuuu" sound about six inches from a student's ear. Encourage the student to "oouuuuu" along with you. Make no comment on accuracy. Then move to the other ear and repeat the "oouuuuu" sound.

- Ask the student to close his or her eyes and repeat the same exercise with both ears.

- Ask the student to look at the tip of your finger (which you hold about 8"–12" in front of the student's nose). Repeat the "oouuuuu" sound toward each ear.

In *Rhythms of Learning* on pages 39, 40, and 41, there are many more exercises that will assist you in discovering which ear is the better tonal ear.

24 *Just One More Time*

Rote learning has not been in vogue for the past decade, yet it is true that we need to repeat a pattern a number of times for it to seep down into solid memory. In our gross and fine motor skills, it is necessary to repeat patterns over and over so that facility develops. Multisensory techniques are best. Remember triple-coding. If you wish to sit still, use these very effective variations on NLP techniques.

Whether you are teaching vocabulary, learning foreign words, or reviewing the names of students and clients, this six-step exercise is a winner!

Six-step exercise:

1. Spell and pronounce a foreign word, looking at it on paper in front of you.

2. Repeat with the eyes looking upward to the left.

3. Repeat with the eyes looking upward to the right.

4. Repeat with the eyes looking downward to the left.

5. Repeat with the eyes looking downward to the right.

6. Repeat slowly with the eyes closed.

25 *Where in the World Are YOU ?*

Sometimes we take our environment and teaching rooms as they are without questioning the best ways to arrange them. Take a quick check of the following.

- Are there many outside sounds?

- From which direction do they come?

- Does the heating or air conditioning make a constant sound?

- Do the lights make sound?

We know how difficult it is to read when sitting at a desk facing out a window, and we naturally would change the desk's position. Sound sources have just as much impact on memory and general well-being (and relaxation) in the classroom.

Position the class away from noise sources. Allow students' bodies and leading ears to be seated so heads do not have to turn when listening to you. Put noise sources (traffic, lights, air vents) on the left ear side of students. Move listeners who have attention problems or those who have to strain to listen closer to your right side.

26 *JUST TOO LOUD*

Loud music can coagulate eggs; strong, directed frequencies can break glass; and slow baroque music can improve the growth of plants. Sounds instantly are measured in the body through muscle tension, skin temperature, heartbeat, and breath patterns. Sound pollution can create serious problems physically and mentally.

If there is a constant sound in your office or classroom, chances are high that your brain masks it. After awhile you stop hearing it. But your body and brain must compensate for this luxury ability in your consciousness. Some constant sounds create high blood pressure, drowsiness, lack of concentration, and sometimes just a constant emotional irritation.

Survey your work environment and notice the loud sounds. Actually, if you will just sit in the room for ten minutes with no one there, you may realize that the seemingly quiet lights and air movement are very, very loud. By changing light bulbs and adjusting air vents, you may be able to alter your environment instantly.

27 *Enough Is Enough!*

The following exercises contain many suggestions for using music in a learning or study environment. But take note: too much use of music is almost like no music. The optimal use of sound and music is about twenty minutes per hour. The brain and body adjust to everything after a while and begin to "habituate." Then the music serves no use at all.

Vocal patterns and general thinking activities are best inspired by seven minutes of interlude when the teacher intuitively senses a lull in attention.

Without stopping a class, put on a piece of slow Baroque music about twenty minutes after the class has started. Many cassette albums only have twenty to twenty-five minutes of music per side. Place the cassette deck or speakers to your far right as you face the room so that this quiet music does not immediately catch the attention of the listeners' dominant (right) ears.

28 *Attitudinal Music*

Dr. Arthur Harvey has spent years researching the effect of music on people's attitudes. He realized that light music in the background creates an environment just as much as the air quality, light quality, and temperature. By using pieces of music that are four or five minutes in length, it's possible to create the most positive learning environment for a class.

As students enter a classroom, play softly a cassette recording of baroque, classical, new age, or light jazz music (no vocal music). Be sure the cassette turns off after five minutes. Begin class as you speak over the music. Be sensitive—don't overexcite or relax the students too much.

29 CHARGE! The Miracle Tapes

Many people have collections of tapes, records, and CDs that contain their favorite music. Find several three- to five-minute pieces of music that awaken you, delight you, and make you feel good. Play a selection in your car, office, or the classroom for a short "sound break." Caution: Use this technique only for charging and activating your interests. If you play all the pieces in one sitting, this method will lose its effectiveness.

Here are some of my own selections:

- Bach, *Well-Tempered Clavier*, Prelude in D Major
- Mannheim Steamroller, *Saving the WildLife*, "Amanda Panda"
- March for the Olympic Games
- Sousa, "The Stars and Stripes Forever"
- Brahms, *Hungarian Dances*

30 *Calm-Down Miracle Music*

This is the same technique as used in the previous exercise. This time find music that soothes and gently relaxes you. You'll want only five minutes of tape that is not too slow—otherwise you'll go to sleep. You may want to test your selection during sound breaks in class.

Don's Calm-Down Selections:

- Debussy, "The Maid with the Flaxen Hair"
- Bach, *Well-Tempered Clavier*, Preludes in C Major and B Minor
- Burt Bacharach, "Raindrops Keep Falling on My Head" (soundtrack from *Butch Cassidy and the Sundance Kid*)
- "My Favorite Things" from *The Sound of Music*
- "Amazing Grace" (traditional spiritual)
- classical guitar music

31 *From Microphone to Macrophone*

When I first visited the Tomatis Center in Paris, I noticed that some of the children and adults were listening to their own voices with their right hands up to their chin as if they were holding a microphone or an ice cream cone. Later I learned that using this hand position significantly "charges" the voice.

Give children a microphone to pass around when they wish to speak. There is an automatic image of their voice being amplified, of really being heard. For presentations or recitations, such as a poem, have a "talking stick" that is held by the right hand (even if the student is left dominant) so there is a physical tool to hold. At home you can practice with your own "talking stick."

32 *Getting to Work*

In this society of commuters, we often have more time for special activities during rush hour than at any other time of day. I've often been told that the commuting time is a favorite time of day because it affords a unique kind of privacy, away from work and family.

It's easy to forget how useful this time can be. The following exercise, done on your way to work, can open the voice and charge the brain. It's filled with natural, vibratory caffeine.

For two minutes, the sound of "eeeee" will massage your scalp, mind, and body. Without any strain to the face, jaw, or throat, just exhale the "eeee" sound. Allow it to flow upward and downward and to vibrate the head. It will charge your day, clear your voice, and surely keep negative thoughts away. (Self-consciousness can set in for the first day or two, but after you realize the benefits, the exercise might grow to ten minutes of joyous sounding.)

33 *It Was Just One of Those Days*

Driving home, we are sometimes tired, sometimes stressed by the pressures of the day and perhaps by emotions that may not have been expressed. The voice can release, charge, and balance out our inner stress within a couple of minutes.

The tape *Heal Yourself with Your Own Voice* is loaded with suggestions.

Begin to speak with emotions, almost without words. Review the day in your mind and let your voice simply express the pleasure, tension, joy, or boredom of the different parts of the day. Concentrate on your throat and shoulders and notice which sounds release the tension there. This is a great exercise when you are driving alone in traffic.

34 *The Hum*

This may sound like the emperor's new ears, but humming is an efficient, quick, and inexpensive integrator! Within two minutes humming can center the brain waves, release stress from the body, and charge the voice. Humming is best done with the lips closed and the jaw and chin relaxed. It works well in subways, airplanes, loud restaurants. It's great for a moment or two while walking down the hall or on the elevator. It is a very private event that can rescue even the most boring moments.

Start with a very quiet humming sound, something like an internal "ah." Then think of charging this quiet sound with power. At first you may get louder, but soon you can notice that it can be robust, clear, and interesting without too much volume. This helps before presentations, between long conversations, during lectures, or in the middle of telephone calls. (I've even held the phone to my right ear and hummed for two minutes—a great sound break!)

35 I'll Try Anything Once

We have babbling brains that inhibit our actions and just won't turn off. There are days when I can't hear myself think because of all the thoughts! Toning is a simple and great way to clear the inner thought, get centered and grounded, and proceed with insight and vigor.

When you feel overloaded by the internal "stuff" and need a real clearing, find a place where others won't hear you and get out the sonic window cleaner.

This is a fifteen-minute sound cleansing. You'll never know how much tension and "unsaid" stuff is held in the body until you try this exercise or get a massage on Friday afternoon. Close your eyes and start to make any vowel sound for four or five minutes, then change it into a really powerful "ay-yai-yaiiiiiiii," "Wheeeeee," or "Yo, yo, yo, yo," and let the sounds keep flowing naturally. Your left brain will think you've somehow sown the last seed, but the midbrain and the body will begin to release sounds naturally. A few primordial screams may occur at first, but if you continue this exercise for a couple of days, the most wonderful lulling sounds and comforting sounds will start to emerge.

36 *Mouth Sounds*

Fifteen years ago, I had no idea what the range and the power of the voice was. I had studied voice in college and then taught speech, reading, and choral music, but I had never unleashed my natural voice.

It was not until I was given some very curious tapes that I was stunned by the power of the voice. I heard people singing two, three, and even four notes at a time. I heard a voice that could sing a chord on the bottom and an independent melody on top. I heard some very strange languages (clicking African tongues) and more varieties of sounds than I could imagine.

Dr. Tomatis points out that each language or dialect actually modifies posture and attentiveness.

Here's an album that will charge your listening ear with delicious folk sounds and languages of another time. *Mouth Music** is a collection of Gaelic folk tunes performed with African rhythms. It is full and robust. It's a great sing-along album and excellent for playing at the beginning of a class. It gets everyone's attention.

You can find it in good record shops. If not available, ask for Paul Winter's *Earth Beat* or the Bulgarian Women's Choir singing *Le Mystére des Voix Bulgares.*

* Martin Swan and Talitha Mackenzie, *Mouth Music* (Rykodisc cassette, Triple Earth Music 0196, 1991).

37 Toning Up Your Body, Tuning Up Your Mind

Toning is the vocal elongation of a vowel sound. By staying on a relaxed sound for a couple of minutes at a time, you can massage, invigorate, and release stress in many parts of the body.This is one of those exercises that you'll adapt to your own creative needs. Five minutes in the morning and five in the evening can bring on radical attacks of joy, relaxation, and creativity.

Sit comfortably with your eyes closed and concentrate on relaxing your jaw. Begin with a minute of an "ah" sound and release stress in the throat and shoulders. Then change to an "oooooh"sound and feel the center of the chest and heart area open and feel charged. Then make a long "hay" sound and let it massage your face and charge the mind with energy. Then spend a minute on "whee" and let it roll all over the head, changing pitch. Explore how it can free up the mind and release mental stress. That's it! Be ready for a great day.

At the end of the day, reverse the order of this exercise and you'll be ready to rest.

38 *Change Your Voice, Change Your Mind*

Your voice indicates what is going on in your mind and in your body. At the Institute for Music, Health and Education we have been studying the effects of the voice on the body and how every vocal sound is loaded with important information about the health of the mind, emotions, and body. As the body can change the voice, so the voice can actually change the body and the emotions. It's a two-way street.

Once you begin to listen to your voice in a variety of ways, you'll be able to detect what is missing and what can be done to harmonize yourself. It is not necessary to develop loud or dramatic sounds to make significant changes. Just adding subtle new patterns into the voice and ear changes the vibratory energy that carries information and emotion through speech.

Pay attention to two of your voices: the everyday, typical patterned voice and the charged, enthusiastic voice. When teaching, notice when your voice becomes charged and powerful.

Now pay attention to the conversations and responses of those around you. Is the voice emotional, bored, inhibited, breathy, clear? How does a specific voice change day by day? When working with children, spend thirty minutes speaking with a Spanish, German, or French accent. See how your change of voice changes the state of mind.

39 *Don't Worry If You Can't Sing!*

Somewhere along the line a teacher may have told you that you could not sing, that you could not carry a tune. Well, the good news is: you still have full vocal power. Actually, we've discovered that everyone with ears can match tones and pitches within a couple of minutes. Yes, EVERYONE. Most music teachers do not know that the position of the eyes determines pitch. They may not be aware that much of sound identification is through bone conduction rather than air conduction. Voice teachers may not be updated on ear dominance and may not know that one ear usually tunes better than the other one.

Be forgiving and patient with yourself. There is hope! You may not be born to be Caruso, but there is at least a Bob Dylan and perhaps a Willie Nelson in you!

Review the six positions of the eyes in exercise 24. Have a friend make a long "eee" sound about a foot from your right ear. Sound the pitch you feel and hear (without being critical or judgmental). There are six different pitches for the different positions of the eyes!

Now do the same with the sound stimulus on the other side of your face, dominating the other ear. This is a great way to help a child find his or her tonal voice. At this stage, it's not necessary to inhibit the voice with judgment, just keep exercising this form of listening and matching.

40 *Both Sides Now*

Most of us have developed a true dominance through movement on one side of our body. Even though I can play the piano well with both hands, my left hand has never been a good writer. The brain and body are grateful for some specific attention on the nondominant side. This little exercise is easy and can wake up some of the least used parts of the brain.

Put on some active music: the theme from *Flashdance,* a German polka, or a fast movement from *The Nutcracker,* for example. Write your name with your nondominant hip five times, then with your nondominant elbow, then the whole head and then both hands. Spell vocabulary words, review key concepts, get exercise, lose weight, stay awake, and have fun all at once!

41 *Brilliant Babble*

Remember visiting Europe or Mexico where everyone spoke a foreign language? At first it seems impossible to understand and communicate, and then the creative kid takes over. You slow down, use hand gestures, try intuitive charade techniques—and somehow major questions get resolved.

Tongues and mouths are usually very inhibited about making sounds that seem not to have a specific meaning or emotion. Yet we are loaded with the ability to make sense out of nonsense sounds. This exercise is one of the most challenging and most helpful. It opens up language and listening centers of the brain.

Just begin to babble. Think of some very creative and unlikely phrase—"What is for lunch today at the fire station, Fred?" Then translate it into intuitive French, then German, then Russian, then Egyptian, and then in a new language. Make up feelings, inflections, and vocabulary for each language and notice how your posture, voice, and thought patterns change.

42 *Improving the Listening Environment*

If you have been doing every one of the previous exercises in consecutive order, you have already reached a state of well-being. But just in case you bought this book to learn about using music in your teaching environment, you can start here. The next dozen or so exercises will let you know the power of different styles of music and how they affect your teaching.

These exercises are written for you. By the time you experiment with each style of music, you will have developed an intuition that lets you choose the ideal music to match your teaching style.

The next exercises will experiment with music of many styles and periods. You may not have examples of these sounds in your own library, so this will assist you in buying new tapes. Begin with any piece of music you like that does not use voice or words. We want to let the music speak. Then, stand or sit with your eyes closed and just listen to the language in the music. You may see an image or a story develop. You may hear the melody as if it were sentences in a foreign language. You may wish to translate it or just listen to it for its natural expression. Get used to being a noncritical music listener.

43 *Getting Comfortable*

Three or four minutes of relaxation is helpful for optimizing learning. It is most useful after a high-stress day. Using headphones at the school or office, or your stereo system at home, is best. Specific suggestions for listening in your car will come later. This exercise is preparation for teaching or learning. It is not for deep rest or sleep, unless you deserve that rest and your body insists on a nap.

Close your eyes and exhale. Let the sounds gently release tension in your body. Daydream a little and know that after five minutes you'll stretch, move, and feel refreshed.

Sound Suggestions (not too slow, music with melody):

- Eric Satie, *Trois Gymnopédies* (piano music)
- Don Campbell (arrangements), Cosmic Classics (light classical music)
- Paul Winter, Sunsinger (beautiful soprano saxophone music)
- Claude Debussy, "Claire de Lune"

44 *Catnap Time*

Napping after lunch is a normal inclination for small and very large children. Reading a story, or allowing eight to ten minutes for complete permission to rest can save a full afternoon from being groggy. At the end of this deep rest, it's important to have a sparkling or active piece of music to motivate the mind and refresh the body.

Find a very comfortable posture, close the eyes, and begin to exhale tension and thoughts. Know that this is a ten-minute rest and refreshment time, not a full afternoon's nap. Concentrate on release and refreshment.

Sound Suggestions (very slow music with elongated melodies):

- Samuel Barber, "Adagio for Strings"
- Don Campbell, *Runes*, side 1 (deep relaxation composition)
- Don Campbell, *Tranquility* (soft music for deep breathing)
- Adagio album from *Relax with the Classics*

 *Bright and Shiny*

There is nothing like a minute or two of bright, stimulating sounds. This sound break has made study and learning interesting for many hours. Every hour or two a "bright and shiny" break can be equal to a cup of coffee and a walk around the block.

In a seated posture, close your eyes and exhale deeply three or four times. As the music begins, see yourself jogging, dancing, or conducting the music.

Sound Suggestions (clear, melodic music with a fast pace, yet not frantic):

- The Cambridge Buskers (Deutsche Grammophon). All of their albums, using pennywhistle and little accordion, are bright arrangements of fine music.

- Mannheim Steamroller, *Saving the Wildlife* (a wondrous collection of pieces in a variety of styles)

- Bach, many of the preludes from *Well-Tempered Clavier*

- Sousa marches

46 *Pay AT-Tension*

What a strange word, *attention*. To tense up has been basic to learning and listening for a long time. Actually, it is not completely off center for learning. Muscles relax more when they are first made tense. Controlling the relaxation from a tense state is a technique and a pattern that is useful to practice. Too much continual "at tension" creates stress, inhibition, and long-range physical problems.

Here are some musical suggestions that help get attention and bring the body into a sharper alignment. Note: a little goes a long way!

Sound Suggestions (dynamic, powerful, sometimes rhythmic):

- March for the Olympic Games
- 20th Century Fox theme song
- Theme from *Rocky*
- Air force theme, "Off we go . . ."

47 *Intricate, Complex, and Interesting*

One of the greatest marvels of the mind is its ability to think in complex systems simultaneously. That sometimes happens with a busy secretary who answers phones, writes letters, sends out mailings, and is a receptionist . . . or with the housewife who cooks, organizes a neighborhood event on the phone, feeds the dog, and cares for two children at the same time. Great business leaders, heads of corporations, airline pilots, and symphony conductors are a few of the many who are required to concentrate on several things simultaneously.

Bach was the greatest composer of intricate, contrapuntal music. He could write a theme and play it in four or five ways in different rhythms, and in many voices at the same time. He composed melodies that were played backward and forward at the same time. By listening to Bach, the logical, linear, and complex mind comes to attention.

Sound Suggestions (all by Bach):

- Little Fugue in G Minor for Organ
- The Jig Fugue
- The Two-Part Inventions for Piano or Clavier
- The D Major Fugue for Organ

48 *Emotional Drain and Overflow*

Daily and weekly it's helpful to have an "emotional time." Dedicate five minutes to feeling and releasing tension or just plain clearing up the feelings. Being emotional does not mean being sentimental or having a quick reaction to everything. Emotion is the connection between feelings and actions.

Sometimes there is too much emotion to be released by physical movement and music. Sometimes there is little emotion and a need to open the heart feeling center. Use your voice to hum, shout, sing, or just improvise as the music plays.

Sound Suggestions:

- To release emotions—theme from *Flashdance*
- To emote feeling—soundtrack from *The Mission*

49 Movie Creator

At times, just plain daydreaming is important. With a little help from music, we can reach safely into the creative depth of our unconscious mind. Every five or six months, I take an hour to listen to orchestral music without words to observe the pictures and stories that are available from my intuitive mind. Without an intention, for relaxation and pleasure, sit back, listen, and "watch" what's happening in the music.

This kind of simple exercise is best followed by a little catnap, then writing some of the story or ideas that emerged through the music. Drawing with pastels, walking, and singing, or just sitting quietly, can be fruitful after watching your sound movie.

Sound Suggestions (20 minutes of colorful, emotive music from the romantic or impressionist periods):

- Music for imaging—a full side from *Relax with the Classics*

- Smetana, *The Moldau*

- Debussy, *La Mer*

- Tomita, Snowflakes Are Dancing (synthesizesd Debussy)

- Mahler, Symphony No. 1, first movement

50 *Gregorian Plus (600–1400)*

Some of the earliest music in Western civilization is some of the most important. The beautiful and lyric chant that was developed by Pope Gregory around the year 600 is being used to release stress and quiet classrooms and is even sung in a few elevators in the corporate world. Since Vatican II, some Japanese, Methodists, Buddhists, and even psychotherapists have used Gregorian chant for many reasons. Chant was the basis for all music for nearly eight hundred of the years following its origin. Here's a chance to enjoy the blessed spirit of sound to ease and soothe your day.

The golden treasure of sound in Western music is held in these vibrant, smooth, and mellow vocal sounds of Gregorian chant. They are ready to soothe and inspire.

Sound Suggestions:

- Gregorian sampler—*The Monks of Solesmes*, Paraclete Records

- Vespers and complines—*Solesmes*, Paraclete Records

- Doctors and bishops—*Solesmes*, Paraclete Records

- Chant—*The Healing Power of Voice and Ear* by Tim Wilson. This is a magical documentary on the work of Dr. Tomatis and chant! (From the Institute for Music, Health and Education.)

51 *Renaissance Ready (1400–1600)*

Creativity blossomed overnight during the Renaissance. Music, art, thought, and architecture were given glorious expression. Fine instrumental music blended with folk styles. The pageantry and inspiration of vocal music brought wondrous delight to the human spirit.

This wonderful music is not as well known as the other periods of music. Some sounds a little distant from our everyday musical sounds. But here are some ideas for building a good library of sound.

Sound Suggestions:

- Renaissance band music (marches and dances)
- Spanish dances of the Renaissance
- The "greatest hits" of the Renaissance

Go to a well-stocked classical record store in your area and ask for one of the experts! Renaissance albums come and go and the titles and availability may change.

52 Go for Baroque
(1600–1750)

Every period of music has a variety of styles, instrumentations, and sounds. The baroque period has become very popular in accelerated learning methods because of its poetic and almost linguistic forms. Some of the primary composers of that period were Bach, Handel, Pachelbel, Telemann, Corelli, Purcell, Monteverdi, and Albinoni.

Slow movements of baroque music are most effective in creating study, listening, and concentrating learning situations. The baroque period produced a lot of fast, fiery, and celebrational music. Remember Bach's Toccata and Fugue in D Minor, which is used by nearly every horror show organist? That's not great for concentrated study.

Getting to know baroque music is easy and enjoyable; a wide variety is available. Baroque can be great while driving the car and excellent for setting up a good study atmosphere.

Sound Suggestions:

- *Zamfir plays Baroque Favorites on the Panpipes.* This Phillips Recording is one of my all-time-never-get-tired-of favorites!

- Bach's "greatest hits"

- Pachelbel's "greatest hits"

- Handel's *Water Music*, flute concertos, harp concertos

- Telemann's flute concertos

53 *Isn't It All Classical? (1750–1820)*

Even though I studied music at the Paris Conservatory of Music and have degrees in organ and music education, my parents thought I played only classical music. To them Bach and Debussy were classical composers and they enjoyed classical music as long as they didn't have to sit through long performances of Bruchner and Wagner (who were not classical composers).

Confused? It's a bit awkward to give mini-history lessons every time the word *classical* is used, especially when we mean the *classical period*. If we took a vote, we might just change the name of that period of music to the Haydn–Mozart period.

The freedom of form of the baroque period became strict in the classical period. The forms (symphony, sonata, and concerto) developed and matured in that time. New emotional expressions were used. For more information call your local music teacher!

The joy of real classical music is its clarity, elegance, and transparency. Dr. Tomatis believes Mozart wrote the healthiest music in the world because it rhythmically and harmonically stimulates essential patterns of brain growth. (See my books *Rhythms of Learning* and *Music: Physician for Times to Come* for details on Dr. Tomatis.)

Sound Suggestions:

- Mozart's or Haydn's "greatest hits"
- Mozart's most popular symphony movements
- Highlights from Mozart operas

54 What's This Romantic Stuff? (1820–1910)

Romantic music includes the articulate symphonic expressions of Schubert and Schumann, the imaginative and colorful music of Tchaikovsky, the brilliant music of Chopin, Liszt, and Paganini, the operas of Puccini and Verdi, and the creations of hundreds of other composers.

Music in Western culture has evolved and integrated forms and styles from all previous periods, so symphonies, concertos, operas, sonatas, fugues, ballades, ballets, suites, and tone poems are scattered everywhere. Early romantic composers sound classical; late romantic composers are considered post-romantic and impressionist.

Romantic does not mean sweet, sentimental, or sugar-filled (even though Tchaikovsky had a sweet tooth). Rather, there is an emphasis on expression and feeling. Individualism, nationalism, and mystical subjects were very popular in the romantic period.

You can sit back and enjoy the power of imagination with the late romanticists' tone poems like Richard Strauss's *Also Sprach Zarathustra* or Smetana's *Moldau*. Or just sit and watch the glorious colors of Bizet's opera *Carmen*—fine music for creative thinking or projects! Some students and teachers are just listeners and may not wish to blend romantic listening with study!

Sound Suggestions (a large selection of many styles from the nineteenth century) include:

- "Greatest hits" from the romantic period
- Themes from Tchaikovsky, *Swan Lake* and symphonies
- Chopin preludes
- Schubert symphonies
- The romantic list is so long that it makes up most of the "classical" section in many record stores.

P.S. The census bureau noticed that the population increased more in the romantic period than during any previous period in the history of music!

55 Let's Make an Impression
(turn of the century)

One day a young composer, Claude Debussy, was walking in a public park in Paris during the great world exhibition when he heard a gamelon orchestra from Indonesia. The sounds and musical rhythms were from another world. Those sounds inspired his romantic expression and the beginning of the impressionist movement. Debussy and Ravel created some of the most etheric and sensitive music of all time during the first decades of the twentieth century.

Piano interludes are always helpful in a learning environment. Here are some of the most useful and beautiful.

Sound Suggestions (piano music of Debussy):

- Preludes (vol. 1), includes: "Footsteps in the Snow" and "The Maid with the Flaxen Hair"

- Children's Corner Suite

- Arabesques 1 and 2

- Suite Bermasque, which includes "Claire de Lune"

56 Contemporary Means Everything *(from 1915–eternal Now)*

Every period of music, when it is current, is contemporary. I'll be pleased in the year 2000 when suddenly "contemporary" music will be history and we can speak of the surviving twentieth-century music with pride. My guess is that the twentieth century will be divided into more periods and styles than any other century.

In any case, the sounds and power of Stravinsky, Shostakovich, Copland, and Gershwin are truly worthy of a weekend of listening for every teacher, trainer, and student.

Four albums will give you ample ideas for imagery, expression, release, and enjoyment. You'll find some important uses for them in class!

Sound Suggestions:

- Stravinsky, *Rite of Spring* or *Sacre du Printemps*. It is a ritual cleansing of all left-brain matters.

- Dimitri Shostakovich, Symphony no. 5. This Russian composer has captured all the energy, elegance, and complexity of the mid-century in this work. Leonard Bernstein's recording is still the masterpiece.

- Aaron Copland, *Appalachian Spring* and *Billy the Kid* are standards for imagery in the classroom. Very American!

- George Gershwin, "Rhapsody in Blue"—standard American masterpiece for piano and orchestra.

Pop, Rock, and Rap

A few years ago we could have classified all these terms with specific examples, but during this last decade of the century these styles, along with folk and classical styles, are fusing. That makes it confusing!

Elvis, the Beatles, and Michael Jackson have made their repetitive and rhythmic mark on the soul of world music. The important use of rhythmic patterns truly does affect the basic patterns of the brain. The development of movement and the need to make verbal, tonal sounds are important in the growth of the body and brain.

Elvis, Ringo, and Michael have hit home to the hindbrain, the autonomic brain, and the reptilian systems. They are our ancestors and support all the higher brains, so let's get up and move once a week to the beat! (Music should be loud enough for the body to feel, but soft enough for the ears to be safe!)

Sound Suggestions:

- Dance and sing with the theme from *Flashdance*

- Lip-sync Elvis's "Hound Dog"

- Every five years, listen to the Beatles' "Sgt. Pepper's Lonely Hearts Club Band" with a friend and philosophize on how it changed your life and society!

58 New Age Ars Nova Music (1300–2001)

Radical new music started to be composed in the fourteeth century. Later it was called the "ars nova" or "new arts." There was so much happening that suddenly (new arts) music that was not sacred started to sound sacred. There was new rhythmic freedom and a revolt against music in triple meter. In France and Italy, people began to write music on paper. This period was the seeding for the Renaissance. (Close your eyes and imagine how awesome things were in 1344.)

New age music may have ambiguous melodies, no rhythmic design, and lots of "spacy" images, but it is seeding an important new concept of sound: that space, environment, and time can be modified by tone and rhythm; that health can be improved with spacious, colorful sounds; and that everybody in the universe can make a cassette album with no training! These are part of our "ars nova."

Some wonderful ambient music is available. I enjoy composing in this new style with all sorts of combinations of tones and dichotic techniques (each ear gets different sounds). Use these sound suggestions for relaxation, meditation, imagery, and other quiet activities.

- Brian Eno, *Ambient One: Music for Airports* (Celestial Arts). Excellent for study and relaxation.

- Jonathan Goldman, *Dolphin Dreams* (Spirit Music). Image how heartbeats, dolphins, ocean tides, and a choir with three notes can really be interesting, restful, and quieting!

- Don Campbell, *Crystal Meditations* (Spirit Music). A composition based on soothing brain-wave patterns, tonal patterns, and breath; "field-tested" album good for low beta waves and relaxation.

59 Country and Eastern Music

It won't be long before Dolly Parton and Ravi Shankar make an album together! Styles and moods are blending. In graduate school, I wrote a paper on south Indian classical (watch out—there's that word again) music. Most of my professors were not aware that there are more than 4,000 scales, rhythmic modes, and defined moods in Indian music. Two of my music education teachers swore to "major and minor," "happy and sad" as the only two emotions music could express.

There is great wisdom in every style of music, whether it is familiar or not. Give yourself a "sound break" with these great albums.

Sound Suggestions:

- Ravi Shankar and Yehudi Menhuin, *East Meets West* (Angel)

- Ravi Shankar, Morning or Evening Ragas

- Dolly Parton, Linda Ronstadt, and Emmylou Harris, *Trio* (Warner Brothers). If you've never given country a chance, this is a good way to start.

P.S. Have you seen the "New Age Business Card"? It lists more than a dozen professions with the ancient, modern, and next-life names, includes telephone, fax, modem numbers, astrological data, blood type, brain-wave patterns, six religious beliefs, and is carried in an organic, plastic, imaginary card holder!

60 *How to Use All That Jazz*

Jazz means blues, gospel, Dixieland, soul, Brubeck, wild improvisations, sax, and dozens of other styles. It grew out of personal expression, survival, and that unending release of joy and sadness that music creates when it comes from the spontaneous heart.

Nearly everyone has favorite jazz pieces. But if we compared the styles and artists, we'd find another world of fusion. In the 1950s it was easy to organize jazz, but more recently it's been influenced by Africa, opera, and athletics.

Here are some not-to-be-missed light jazz favorites, great for sound breaks in conferences, classrooms, or the car.

Sound Suggestions:

- Claude Bolling, *Suite for Flute and Jazz Piano* (CBS)

- Dave Brubeck, *Take Five* (Columbia)

- Bill James, *One* (CBS)

- *Claude Bolling's Greatest Hits* (CBS)

61 Earth Music from Everywhere

In New York, Los Angeles, London, Tokyo, Boulder, and even Alvin, Texas, there are record sales and concerts by artists from all over the world. Just reading the arts section of a Sunday paper helps us realize that we do live on a planet of interesting sounds.

New styles, new instruments, and new integrated sounds will emerge in the twenty-first century. Both the refined, unique, local quality of folk music and the integrated "designer sound" will be there for our great grandchildren.

Look for great tastes in new styles for the ears. Hold on for fun! These are good sound breaks for the class, car, or gathering and are easy ways to travel to all the ears of Earth.

Sound Suggestions:

- Paul Winter, *Earthbeat* (Living Music). Russian folk, new age sax, light jazz, and a heart of gold!

- Kitaro, *Silk Road*. This Japanese heart man blends synthesizer, new age, and soft jazz into peaceful, Oriental, Western melodies. Kitaro himself is as gentle and kind as his music.

- Vangelis, *China* (Polydor). My favorite Vangelis album blends East, West, North, South, poetry, and space into this colorful album. This world-class musician does not like to travel by air, so his ears take him everywhere.

62 *Compose Myself?*

You may not yet have the ears of Mahalia Jackson, the voice of Maria Callas, the fingers of Horowitz, or the arms of Seiji Osawa, but you are a musician. By sensing your heartbeat, breathing, and humming, you are becoming aware of the inner musician that rhythmically pulses, beats, and tics us through life.

With a cassette tape recorder, take five minutes to record yourself tapping or beating a drum, a table, or a pan. Stay consistent with the basic beat. That's what foot tapping is for! Play it back and just close your eyes and start to hum, click, hiss, or sing along without thinking. Do this daily for a few weeks and listen to what happens naturally. Heaven knows you may find the great music teacher, after all, inside yourself!

63 I Just Forgot to Breathe

I get into my head, into thought, into a radical symphony of logic, and I forget there are easier ways to learn and be creative. My publisher called me last week and wanted to know if I could write this book now! After thinking of every logical reason for not having time, I started to breathe again.

So, here's a book written with music (Mozart and Claude Bolling) in the background. Using the imagery exercises from *Rhythms of Learning* and *Introduction to the Musical Brain*, I am doing this short breathing exercise every fifteen minutes.

Just plain breathe and count in your head: Inhale 2-3-4-5-6-7-8, hold 2-3-4-5-6-7-8, exhale 2-3-4, hold 2-3-4-5-6-7-8. Do it three times using this pattern, eyes open or closed or in combination. Toning works well too, without counting. Make a long "eehhh" sound, then relax, slowly inhaling, toning, and resting. Recharge and get ready to go!

64 Butterflies in the Throat

Not everyone wants to teach or train. There is a fear of speaking in public. Even some great artists of the concert stage and theatre still get butterflies after years of performance.

Three minutes of toning an "ah" sound in the richer, lower register of your voice will greatly enhance your public speaking voice, release tension, and help you keep calm. Twenty long sounded yawns will work just as well.

65 What Happened to Beethoven, Brahms, and Mendelssohn?

Dr. Georgi Lozanov has developed ways of using romantic, classical, and baroque music during the process of lecturing. His research has shown the benefits of using movements of baroque music for reading and memory enhancement. These "active" and "passive" concerts are very useful tools. They are explained in length in chapter 6 of *Rhythms of Learning*. But here is an exercise that I didn't include in that book.

Practice giving a lesson while playing one of the movements from the following symphonies. Then give the same lesson while a different symphony movement is playing. Let your voice match the emotions of the music. Review the themes of your lessons as the themes (melodies) in the music are reintroduced. The worst thing that could happen in a class would be to hear the comment, "At least the music was good!"

Sound Suggestions:

- Beethoven, Symphony no. 1, no. 4, or no. 8

- Brahms, "Academic Overture" or Symphony no. 1, no. 2, no. 3, or no. 4

- Mendelssohn, Symphony no. 4

66 *Invent a New Language*

Have you ever been just plain stuck? Have you found it impossible to come up with a good idea to get a point across in class? Have you taught a subject so many times that you just can't get revved up for another semester?

This funny little exercise that is full of a lot of babble can unplug the most stopped brain. You may not enjoy the initial deep cleansing effects, but it does work.

Take the key words of a lesson. Take the theme of a lecture and convert all the key words and themes into a new language of your own invention. Write down the twenty key words and then the key theme in your own dialect of Transylvanian, Gibber-drawl, or channeled language from the third ray of Lazania. Then give your talk with these new words to yourself. Now when the lecture is presented to your class, you'll have an inner world of newness.

NOTICE: If you do this exercise in front of other teachers or in corporate headquarters you can almost depend on an early retirement party!

67 Speaking an Unknown Language Fluently

Are you ready for a fun brain exercise and teaser? By using an unknown language, we can translate, articulate, and emotionally release all sorts of creative energies.

Read Hugo Ball's wonderful poem **Karawane** aloud with an African accent, then with a French or British accent, then as if you are very happy, then sad. Have the class then translate the meaning, intuitively, into English.

jolifanto bambla o falli bambla
grossigga m'pfa habla horem

EGIGA GORAMEN

higo bloiko russula huju

hollqkq hollala
anlogo bung
blago bung
blago bung
Bosso Fataka

u uuu u
schampa wulla wussa olobo

hejtatta gorem
eschige zunbada

wulubu ssubudu uluw ssubudu

Tumba ba-umpf
Ba - umf

68 *Tongue Tips*

Now that you have conquered the unexplored linguistic centers of your brain, tongue, and emotions, this should be easy. This dates back to my third-grade music teacher who could not understand my Texas accent when I was singing. So off I went, singing the scale slowly and then quickly, with one phrase repeated over and over and over, until I temporarily stopped liking the tip of my tongue.

Over and over in every imaginable way, speak, sing, rap, and repeat and repeat at many speeds:

"The tip of the tongue tells the tale."

69 *Singing in the Shower*

By now you are a pro in listening, toning, and all sorts of refined neurological acrobatics that free inhibitions and release associations. By developing new patternings of voice and thought with the enhancement of music, you can get back into the joy of flow with sound.

Yes, that's all there is. Sing in the shower, sing in the tub, sing in the car, and just let it happen. Hum, tone, make up new languages, compose, decompose tunes you thought you knew but forgot. Improvise, release, and improve.

70 Voice Spectrum Analysis

Since the mid-1970s a remarkable psychologist, Sandra Seagal, has researched the voice. She has found that the voice is encoded with personality traits that signify mental, emotional, or physical dominance. Although every speaking voice has a basic range, there are very dominant overtones in the mid and high ranges. We all shift notes as we learn to express information, emotion, and physical release through our voices.

As you listen to the voices of your students or associates, begin to sense the spectrum of their vocal sounds. Notice if the pitch of their voices gets higher or lower when they are under stress. Notice if a voice is just "stuck" in a few tonal areas or has a wide variety. Some exercises in this book may assist in helping stuck voices develop more expression and a wider range.

71 *Telegrams and Audiograms*

There are messages coming though our ears all the time—information about feelings, information about information, and information reflecting our physical state of being. Dr. Tomatis has realized that the voice is a direct expression of exactly what the ear can hear. By giving each of his students and clients a "listening assessment" with an audiometer, he can see exactly which frequencies are deficient in the ear's ability to hear, focus, and listen. That information is also reflected in the voice spectograph.

D r. Tomatis's basic theory is that the voice can only reproduce what the ear can hear. Be very sensitive to the voices you hear. Can you detect from the voice a hearing or listening deficiency? If there is a hearing deficiency, it is good to suggest that a hearing analysis be given by an audiologist. Sometimes there is a listening deficiency that differs from a hearing problem. You may have excellent hearing abilities but still have listening problems.

72 *Electronic Ears*

It's time for a miracle story. Dr. Tomatis has realized
that listening, learning, speaking, and writing abilities can
be radically changed by stimulating the ear very lightly
with high-frequency sound waves. He suggests passing
music through a series of filters to the ears and through the
cranial bones for optimal results. This very interesting and
usually very effective program has helped many people
with language and learning problems, including dyslexia,
autism, and attention-deficit syndrome. Many adults have
been assisted in learning foreign languages, developing
speaking skills, and increasing the ability to concentrate.

For information about Dr. Tomatis's work, read *The
Conscious Ear, About the Tomatis Method,* or *Rhythms
of Learning*. There are several hundred Tomatis Centers
throughout the world. (Call (602) 381-0086—The
Sound Listening Center in Phoenix—for information
about the center nearest you.)

---

* Alfred Tomatis, *The Conscious Ear* (Barrytown, N.Y.: Station Hill Press,
  1991).
  Gilmor, Madaule, and Thompson, *About the Tomatis Method* (Phoenix,
  Ariz.: Listening Center Press, 1989).

73 *Silent Speech*

Those who are voice shy may not get this far in the book. But if you do, I've got great news. You can practice all the exercises silently five times before you open your mouth! Rehearse inside if you like.

Amplify your quiet "reading voice," then whisper, then off you go. Let the silence flow into sound. This exercise may not sound profound to you, but try it with a shy first grader and you'll see how effective it is.

74 *Silent Sounds*

One of the greatest miracles of the brain is how we remember sounds, vocal textures, and unique melodies. The variations are subtle, but they make a substantial imprint in our memory. This exercise is a fun way to tune up on the inside.

Think of one of your favorite melodies—anything from "Amazing Grace" to "Anchors Aweigh." Even "Happy Birthday" or the third theme from Mahler's Symphony no. 8 (*Symphony of a Thousand*) will do! Now imagine the melody being played on a saxophone, then on a piano, then a violin, then a pipe organ, then on a whistle in a balloon. Invent new sounds to create the melody. For advanced performance, have one instrument play in one ear and another instrument play in the other ear. (No one will ever know if you creatively cheat!)

75 BrainWORKS

Once or twice in a lifetime, we each find someone who is a miracle worker. I've found two who work in education and have all sorts of insight into the healing, teaching, and creating of childhood education.

Carla Crutsinger started BrainWORKS, a private tutorial school in the suburb of Carrollton near Dallas. There she hires gifted high school students to help learning-disabled children and adults. Every fifteen minutes she shifts the dominant mode of attention, for example, from kinesthetic to visual or auditory. Each child is uniquely tested through SOI (structure of intellect) and prescribed a wonderful, creative way to repattern learning. Carla really knows how to make the brain, body, and heart love learning.

Dr. Dee Coulter in Boulder, Colorado, is an educational philosopher and observer. She's spent many years writing about, researching, and teaching others about the triune brain. She's an expert in Waldorf and Montesorri education and can truly inspire us to educate with music, language, and feeling. She's made dozens of educational tapes about brain development, music, and inner scholarship.

Recall the wondrous teachers you had in school. Close your eyes and sense what it was that made them unique and inspiring. Listen to what they would say to you as you now teach. (Also, if you are interested, write Carla Crutsinger at Brainworks, 1918 Walnut Hill, Carrollton, Texas 75006. Dr. Dee Coulter may be contacted at Coulter Publications, 4850 Niwot Rd., Longmont, CO 80501.)

76 Overtones and Old MacDonald

The voice is full of newly discovered possibilities. It is possible to sing two, three, or even five notes at a time. I've heard people sing a beautiful melody while holding a chord underneath. This is called overtone singing. David Hykes calls it "harmonic singing." I call it intriguing and fascinating.

If you are still fascinated, read chapter 6, "The Overtones of Health," in my book *The Roar of Silence*.

If it's a rainy day, or you have just intuitively turned to this page and you'll try anything once, begin to sing the last part of "Old MacDonald Had a Farm"—yes, the "eeeee, eye, eeeeeee, eye, oh" part. Now slow it down so much that you can hear all the overtones in your voice— slowly, really slowly—between each syllable. Slur it all slowly and extend your listening.

77 *A Hundred Voices in One*

When the power and technique of listening are developed, the ear can begin to hear which frequencies and tones are missing from the voice. When the missing sounds are reintroduced over and over through play, games, storytelling, and music, the ear and the voice begin to renew what has been missing.

To slowly move the voice from high to low and from low to high on a vowel sound allows a mapping of the ear and body to take place. This gliding or glissando with a relaxed sound is one of the great keys to vocal and auditory unfoldment.

Begin by humming low in your voice. Then, like an elevator, begin to ascend to the upper regions of sound. It isn't necessary to stop on any pitches, like a scale. With the relaxed jaw, scan upward, take a breath, then scan down. Sense where the voice is strong, when it skips, and how the sound changes. Scanning three times every morning with stretching is an ideal wake-up exercise.

78 Can't Get a Word in Edgewise

Confession time! I've been told by friends and students that my enthusiasm keeps me from listening sometimes. On the other hand, I know what it's like to have something to say and not be able to find a way to blend it into a conversation.

Whether you are in a class or a conference, during the first few minutes it's helpful to give a few signals for every person to use regarding the basic and important need of getting a word in edgewise.

Two signals have helped me become a better listening teacher. The first is the "time out," where the fingers of one hand are directly in the palm of the other. This means "I've got to drink and drain." I know I have five minutes to move the class into a break time, or the "D and D" person will quietly take care of his or her needs.

The other signal is the thumb to index finger with the hand raised. That means the listener has a question or a comment and I will acknowledge them at the next appropriate time. Often we stop in the middle of a skill to answer and question and it is difficult to regain the momentum. This helps with that kind of interruption.

79 *Watermelon Music*

Remember my Dad, the "pour-it-on man" from Arkansas? He had a few other words of wisdom for me when he played music on his electric organ or guitar. All the songs were in G major, played by ear, using the most thorough hunt-and-peck system ever created.

After hours of listening to him play "Deep Purple" using one chord for the left hand and with nearly every note within an octave of his right hand hoping to be chosen for the melody, I would ask if he needed some help.

He once replied, "I love music and I love watermelons. If someone took all the seeds out of a watermelon and put salt on it for me, I wouldn't love it so much. I just love the way I eat watermelon music."

Listen for the textures of sound around you. Is the sound smooth? Thick? Is a voice silky or coarse? Is a room's sound vibrant and flowing, or is it tight and not moving well? Notice what makes your voice and listening skills perform at their best.

80 *Operational-Concrete-Formal-Postformal Voices*

Piaget was brilliantly correct about the phases of development in every child's educational life. The repetition of skills in the body, the naming of the skills, the logic of the skills, and the full integration of skills develop in a pattern. Sometimes we are weak in one of the areas of development and the voice reflects that weakness.

As you get to know your students or trainees, you may discover that when they are caught off guard and do not know the answer to a question, or they were listening to their inner voice, their voice immediately changes. Sometimes formal processes are a challenge, sometimes the concrete processes are not in order. Review the different levels of developmental procedure and begin to sense what causes the voice to lose its charged power of response.

P.S. For a review of brain growth and developmental skills in the Piagetian system, please refer to *Rhythms of Learning*, pages 150–166.

81 *Walkie-Talkie*

There is hardly time for us to add more activities to our daily schedule. Therefore, this is an exercise for joggers, bikers, and walkers who are up and rhythmically at it with their bodies every morning.

Affirmations are helpful in changing long-term patterns that are ready to transform. Phrases like "I'm becoming a more sensitive listener every day" and "My voice is naturally expressing feeling and clear information to those around me" work well.

Write your own affirmations and repeat them in a dozen different expressions and tonalities as you jog, bike, or walk every day.

82 *Mental Floss and Truth Decay*

The recurrence of communication problems and patterns in our professional lives is an indicator that we need to adjust some of our patterns so that we can optimally use our skills.

Here is a set of "mental flossing" questions about what we think, what we do, and what we think we do:

- Do I make clear statements?

- Do I interrupt myself when I am speaking? In other words, do I introduce new thoughts before I have fully explained the present one?

- Do I take for granted that others have understood me clearly?

- Do I give examples in a variety of sensorial ways?

- Do I review what I have said in a varied pattern so that the information may better integrate within the listener?

If all your answers were clear and precise and honest, you are superhuman! Bravo. Listening, teaching, training, and remembering are always two-way streets. It's the variation in communication that makes work a creative and challenging joy!

83 *Extended Ears*

The refined listening ear is able to focus on one voice and thus allow other sounds to fall into secondary attention. Whether we are listening to the radio in the car or students in a classroom or speaking with friends in a crowded restaurant, our focused attention makes that activity possible.

This exercise is for opening the ears and extending their range of attention. Sit outside with your eyes closed and imagine with every breath that one ear is growing and growing. It is able to hear sounds a block or two blocks away. All sounds at all frequencies are being extended. After five minutes of extending one ear, move the attention to the other ear and repeat the same exercise. Then concentrate on all sounds.

The challenge of this exercise is to calm the inner thoughts, the inner voice, and hear what is really sounding in the outer world. Bring the extended ears inward, and sit quietly.

The goal for this exercise is to be able to extend and retract auditory discrimination skills quickly and effectively.

84 *Synesthesia*

Most artists relate their expression through touch, emotions, hearing, and seeing. The combinations are unique to each individual. As a musician, I see the rhythms and patterns as I hear them. This is not a mystical seeing— it is a mental manner of organizing and perceiving.

Music is visual for me. Art, painting, and sculpture usually give me kinesthetic sensations. And yes, I hear movement. I used to think this was a strange secret I had for learning and perceiving, but now I realize that when the senses instantly connect in conscious thought, we have more intuitive tools for expression.

We admit to only five senses, but I think there are about a dozen at work all the time. They include intuition, emotional senses, and pattern and process sensing. Whenever I've improvised with other musicians, I know the other senses are at work! Every child has them; yet because we have not developed words for them, they go uncultivated as if they do not exist!

List your primary and secondary senses. Invent two new senses and put them into symbols or words. Begin to mix, match, and connect the sensory modes. For example, listen to music for five minutes and see all the sound information as art patterns. (You do not actually see it—it is just a visual intuition.) Then listen to music and smell its textures.

The brain delights in these challenges. Some may not come easily and others may be major gateways for your own creative process and memory development.

85 The Three Voices of Eve, Adam, and Yahoo

We each have a number of voices. Our teaching, informative voice is often used professionally. That's our rational, left-brain, neocortex voice. Our emotional, reflective voice is loaded with feelings, tones, and energy from our midbrain or limbic system. Then there are the grunts and groans that are simply an expression of our physical nature. All of these areas are blended in the voice.

Get to know your three voices. Can you tell them apart? Can you sense when one is not being heard by the other two? When do they all blend?

Tape record yourself as you teach, then tape record your voice as you play with a cat or dog, then record sounds as you wake up or go to sleep, have great pain or pleasure. All the voices are one voice, but each is loaded with wondrous information.

86 To Be Stuck or Unstuck—That Is the Question!

For centuries we have thought that we can do only one thing at a time. Actually, the brain is made to do hundreds of things at a time. Hair and toenail growth happen along with toast digestion, the oxygenation of blood, phone conversations, and soup preparation—oh yes, and watching the kids play outside the window!

To send and receive information at the same time is natural, but we are not specifically trained to improve these techniques. Make a list of professional activities on the left side of a page. Then rehearse that skill or activity on the left side of your consciousness. Make another list on the right side of the paper that includes pleasure and refreshment activities. Close your eyes and sense them on the right side of your brain. Now, inwardly do two activities simultaneously.

Here are some examples for your list:

Side A	Side B
Writing an office memo	Listening to a soft piano
Writing a telephone message	Playing with a puppy
Speaking to a friend about finances	Eating fresh fruit
Teaching a class	Walking in the woods

Now reverse sides. Think of the areas where your sensing may be stuck, or a pattern you wish to change at work. Make double sense of it using this exercise. Watch how your inner rehearsals change the flow of the stuckness.

87 *Try to Remember*

We often remember childhood, youth, and college times through feelings. The feelings connect quickly with pictures, smells, sounds, and physical re-sensations. The teachers, relatives, and friends of the past are still a part of our consciousness. To regain their inspiration we can easily reconnect with them.

Recall three people who have been influential in your life. You may remember a teacher, a grandparent, or a college friend. Close your eyes and sense them. See their clothes, their environment, their movements. Now recall their voices. Listen to them in your imagination as they speak to you. What are the qualities of their voices that make them unique? Hold each voice in a special place in your memory. Can you hear its textures, rhythm, and unique style with your eyes open? Can you read a book and hear each voice reading it? Begin to receive the wisdom of those voices in other important activities in your life.

88 The Greater Spiral—Octave after Octave

The younger the ears, the easier it is to introduce new sounds. This is great for the little ones in our lives. By expressing information and feelings in three levels of the voice, children can integrate and improvise easily. The adult voice has about a three octave range, filled with overtones that are heard well outside the range of the piano. Children find voices with wide ranges very interesting, so bring out the storyteller in you and watch their ears perk up!

Imagine a house that has three floors. Each floor is full of voices. The top floor is full of high, bright joyous voices. The middle floor is full of neat and varied speaking voices, full of information, clarity, and charm. The bottom floor is rich and deep and speaks a little slower than the other voices. That voice comes from the chest! Tell a story and find characters for each voice. Encourage children to speak in all their voices every day with each other and to you.

89 The Most Incredible Experience of a Lifetime

There are things in life that cannot be described. I hope you'll give this exercise to two of your close friends before you read it. There is nothing like experiencing it first! I must credit Dr. Jean Houston for allowing me to have this incredible experience at a workshop about ten years ago.

Two friends stand, one on each side of you. Your eyes are closed. Each one is whispering in one of your ears all the wonderful things they know about you. This is the time to exaggerate possibilities and add creative flair. After four minutes, hold on—you may come out glowing like new! It takes three to do this cosmic tango. Take turns raising your bliss level!

90 *Do You "Should" on Yourself?*

If only . . . I must . . . I should have . . .over and over these thoughts can come racing into our mind. Remorse, guilt, and eternal "shoulding" on our selves make the whole life scene heavy and stuck. Truth, honesty, retracing our steps, dedication to attention, listening, and change are important, and it is right to feel amiss at times. But the old patterns of shoulding are not healthy.

Take two days to notice if you should on yourself or should on others. Make a note to tally every time the word *should* comes to your mind. Note if you use the word with students, colleagues, or family. Put an end to shoulding! It's an old form of mental pollution. Write a few alternatives that ease the "must," "should," and "have to" syndrome.

P.S. Don't feel you shouldn't do this exercise!

91 The Future Is NOW

Only the left brain is caught in a time syndrome. It knows the logical timings of process, pattern, and procedure. The prefrontal lobes know if we don't do something about time management, we will end up pressed for time or with holes in the continuity of our teaching.

Some parts of our brain are not limited by sequential, timed activities. We have access to childhood, old age, youth, and prenatal memories all at once. We are equipped to envision the future: new medications, transportation modes, and foods. The brain is not limited to local time.

Music can easily take us into the future. Blend it with our past, and allow new and creative means for problem solving to arise. This exercise helps us realize what dreams and creative ideas are ready to come to mind.

Write down an area you wish to explore. Then begin to brainstorm with a different voice and with yourself as you put on a favorite piece of music that has a fairly powerful beat. A march, a waltz, a popular piece of dance music, or a tango will do. Put a paper plate on the floor and put a colored circle in the middle of it. Move with the music around the plate.

Stay with the movement and keep talking and moving. You may even record the ideas that come to mind. Then after a focused moving and talking time with music, lie down in silence and allow other intuitive thoughts to emerge.

As strange as this may seem, some major corporations are using similar techniques for developing marketing and product ideas.

92 *Hot Lips*

Back to the basics. If there is no breath or blood flow, sometimes we just can't move energy through our brain and bodies. "Move it or lose it" is a neurological truth. Daily we can maintain neural connections that continuously build new pathways in the brain.

The lips and the tongue are right on the midline. Both sides of the neocortex are stimulated simultaneously. Exercises for these two areas are just now coming into common use for children, stroke patients, and retirees who wish to maintain and strengthen thinking skills.

Practice three minutes of lip buzzing, blowing air through the lips, and repetitive "bah-bah-bah" sounds; then massage the end of the tongue behind the teeth, at the roof of the mouth and on the lips. Keep humming. This is great in the car, in the shower, or pre- or post-lipstick time. This exercise is not considered polite at the dinner table or in church.

93 *Get Smart Slowly with Your Left Brain*

It's time to ground and integrate all these exercises and tidbits with some logical, linear updating. Thinking may be one of the least efficient ways to learn, but it is a great companion for survival in our corporate and educational worlds. Here are some good references on listening, speech, and sound. These four books can help widen your perspective and experience with music and voice.

Sound References:

- *The Listening Book* by W. A. Matthew (Shambhala, 1991)

- *About the Tomatis Method,* by Gilmor, Madaule, and Thompson (Listening Center Press, 1989)

- *The Conscious Ear* by A. A. Tomatis (Station Hill Press, 1991)

- *Listening as a Way of Becoming* by Earl Koile (Regency Books, 1979)

94 *Left-Brain Homework*

The rate at which we are learning about the natural abilities of the brain and how it can be used best is mind boggling. Here are some references that are full of exercises, information, and inspiration.

Sound References:

- *The Possible Human* by Jean Houston (Tarcher, 1983)
- *Music: Physician for Times to Come* by Don Campbell (Quest, 1991)
- *Rhythms of Learning* by Chris Brewer and Don Campbell (Zephyr, 1991)
- *Please Don't Sit on the Kids* by Clare Cherry (David Lake Publishers, 1983)

95 *Mysteries, Miracles, and Theory*

Ancient systems of sound were fundamental in the cultures, religions, and social mores in tribes, races, and regional areas throughout the world. The tonality of language, the sacredness of sound, and its use for rites of passage, initiation, and sacred communication are apparent everywhere. The following may be helpful for those who are interested in this area.

Sound References :

- *Nada Brahma* by Joachim-Ernst Berendt (Destiny Books, 1987)

- *Sounding the Inner Landscape* by Kay Gardner (Cadeceus, 1991)

- *Drumming at the Edge of Magic* by Mickey Hart (HarperCollins, 1991)

96 *Left-Brain Atonement*

Meanwhile, back in the tone, there are books that elaborate on how to release the voice naturally. For more information on singing, toning, and performing, these are handy references. All are full of exercises and creative ideas.

Sound References:

- *The Tao of Voice* by Stephen Chun-Tao Cheng (Destiny Books, 1990)

- *The Roar of Silence* by Don Campbell (Quest Books, 1989)

- *A Soprano on Her Head* by Eloise Ristad (Real People Press, 1989)

97 *For Recovering Intellectuals Only*

There is usually a period of life when we want proof, clarity, and direct methods for all of our mindtime investments. Piaget suggests that during the concrete phase of development in childhood, we should be giving clear, direct, naming instructions. Yet in adulthood we can sense that life is to be lived in intuitive, inventive, creative, healthy, and rational ways. Sometimes not all of these viewpoints agree with each other.

When the rational, linear, research tendencies begin to feel inflexible or defensive, it may be difficult to start using right brain, spontaneous exercises. Yet that is when they are most needed.

When the stuck or defensive place begins to dominate, begin to integrate the question, the mood, or the situation while:

- drawing with soft music in the background

- walking and simultaneously toning or humming

- working in the yard and trying to rap, or rhythmically speak

98 *Sound Drips*

Here's a secret that works for me, and as strange as it seems, every day I find it more effective.

By learning to think a continuous tone, vowel, or sound, there is a modification of how I respond and effectively work in the outer world. There are inner, repetitive sounds that have made some sluggish days clear and some busy days relaxing.

The key words are *peace* and *flow*. It is as much the sound and the energy of the vowels within these words as the meanings that are important. Use *peace* when an energized balance is needed. Use *flow* when relaxation and stress release are necessary. Think the word for as long as thirty minutes at a time while doing other activities. Don't repeat the word, but let a continuous vowel sound flow around. It may be a challenge to keep it going a long time, but it is easy after the body has felt the sound. So try it aloud, then let the silence flow, drip, rise, rinse, and relax!

99 Let the Depths Speak

Jean Houston often tells a story about her childhood visit to Edgar Bergen and Charlie McCarthy. She and her father came into a room where Edgar and Charlie were having a conversation about their independent lives. Charlie was just a wooden dummy, but the deep comments, the awareness, and the clarity of his advice to Edgar were stunning.

Part of our consciousness is ever ready to speak to us from a higher, richer place of wisdom. We do not have to be ventriloquists to successfully communicate within ourselves. But it is helpful to have another voice—a puppet, or a prop—that will allow us to enter into this deep inner conversation using audible words!

Find an old hat or two. Let one hat represent a wise, old, deeply sensitive self that speaks from a wisdom place. Let another hat represent play, sport, and child-like expression. Put the wise hat on the right hand and the sporting, youthful hat on the left hand. Begin to speak and ask questions of each of these parts. Listen carefully to the answers to your questions, dilemmas, and discoveries. Recording these sessions can be enlightening. Five minutes of relaxed music listening before this begins can set the mood!

100 *The Grand Finale– It's Just the Beginning!*

These are a hundred ways to help your creative voice, mind, and intelligence to uniquely orchestrate your teaching and learning styles. Some of these ideas may spark a hundred possibilities for you to develop. See these as seeds, not as methods that are cut and dried. Know that our brains, spirits, and actions have no limit to possibilities and growth. There are no real cul-de-sacs in consciousness, except the ones we create for ourselves. The future will be created for the next generations by our high regard for intuition, creativity, trust, and ethics. What may seem like gimmicks are based on dedicated research of hundreds of teachers, psychologists, musicians, artists, speakers, philosophers and YOU! Any limitation for these possibilities is an illusion, like a flat Earth. Life is a miracle and we are equipped with joy to heal the pains, limitations, and dilemma. Starting with ourselves, we are resonating and orchestrating a peaceful, vibrant, creative, and spectacularly interesting future!

An album awaits to inspire your dreams, those of your students, and those of your corporate associates. Just close your eyes, review your past, dream your future, and know that work and dedication will transform that dream into the real, the possible, and the now.

Sound Suggestion:

- "Space Suite" from the large-screen IMAX films *The Blue Planet* and *The Dream Is Alive*, with music by Micky Erbe and Maribeth Solomon (CDC Records # 1010)